Ffrawn Chain

CRUCIFY ALL AMBITION

By the same author:

Bury all Individualism
Glory in Sacrifice

ASHBURNHAM INSIGHTS:
Baptism in Holy Spirit
Blessing and Cursing
Counselling
Deliverance
Healing
Intercession
Prophecy
Tongues and Explanations

THE DEATH OF SELF: 1

Crucify All Ambition

TIMOTHY PAIN

KINGSWAY PUBLICATIONS
EASTBOURNE

First published 1989

Front cover photo: Tony Stone Photolibrary—London

British Library Cataloguing in Publication Data

Pain, Timothy
Crucify all ambition.
1. Bible–Expositions
I. Title II. Series
220.6

ISBN 0-86065-707-8

Production and printing in Great Britain for
KINGSWAY PUBLICATIONS LTD
Lottbridge Drove, Eastbourne, E Sussex BN23 6NT by
Nuprint Ltd, Harpenden, Herts AL5 4SE

This trilogy was inspired by three of the many Christian leaders who have moulded my life. Two of their lives made me start asking the serious questions which lie behind these books. The life of the third man pointed me towards the answer.

This trilogy is dedicated to that man, the Rt Revd Peter Ball, who personifies the principles set out in these three books more than any other man I know.

Contents

The death of Self

LORD, when the sense of Thy sweet grace
Sends up my soul to seek Thy face,
Thy blessed eyes breed such desire,
I die in Love's delicious fire.
   O Love, I am thy sacrifice;
Be still triumphant, blessed eyes;
Still shine on me, fair suns, that I
Still may behold, though still I die.

Though still I die, I live again;
Still longing so to be still slain;
So gainful is such loss of breath;
I die even in desire of death.
   Still live in me this loving strife
Of living death and dying life;
For while Thou sweetly slayest me
Dead to myself, I live in Thee.

A Song of Divine Love
Richard Crashaw

Introduction

When I began writing this trilogy I thought that the material would form volumes nine to twelve in the developing *Ashburnham Insights* series. I set out to write four short books on vision, community, worship, and service, intending to suggest in them that God wants to move us on from personal to corporate renewal, and that we should join Paul in asking to share in the sufferings of Christ as well as in the power of his resurrection. But somewhere between conception and parturition God, and an editor, intervened.

The first eight volumes in the *Ashburnham Insights* series were my attempt at a serious re-reading of Scripture on topics which, currently, are immensely popular. But as I began preparing this new material I realised that I was now focusing on subjects which people prefer to ignore.

When the material for volumes one to eight in the *Ashburnham Insights* was tested in public it received an enthusiastic welcome: some folk may have struggled with small details, but most people endorsed the general principles. However, I am afraid that this new material has gone down everywhere like the proverbial lead balloon.

One summer's evening in 1987, after a particularly violent and antagonistic reception at a Shropshire Bible

Week, I decided that enough was enough. I could not face any more vituperation and decided to ditch the material. But a few quiet words of encouragement and endorsement on the following day from the Rev Frank Cooke gave me the determination to press on and begin pounding my word-processor. So blame Frank if you find this trilogy unpalatable!

I prepared some rough manuscripts, sent them to my editor, and then flew to South Africa where I spent a month living with black clergymen, teaching them, visiting their congregations, and tasting apartheid at first-hand. It was a deeply challenging experience. After South Africa I spent some time in Northern Ireland. And it was there, gazing at the poppy-clad memorial to *Our Glorious Dead* in bomb-scarred Enniskillen, that I began to perceive the common theme which ran through my rough manuscripts.

I arrived home from Ireland to find an encouraging letter from my editor. He stated that some people would be so unhappy with what I had written, and find it so unwelcome, that he didn't know what to do with the manuscripts. After prayer, thought, reflection and discussion we finally agreed not to include this material in the *Ashburnham Insights*, but to develop it into the format of this trilogy.

I belong to that part of the church which is unashamedly both evangelical and charismatic. But in South Africa I was appalled to discover that apartheid appears to have as strong a grip on the lives of evangelical charismatics as it does on members of the armed forces. Certainly that is the view of most of the black Baptist clergymen with whom I stayed in the Transvaal townships.

It would have been easy for me to return home and denounce the white-led charismatic mega-churches of Johannesburg. But I suspected that if I had grown up there I would probably have been part of them, for they emphasised many of the things I hold most dear. They were not bad, but blind. They had a splinter called apartheid in both eyes. And I realised that if I was to take Matthew 7:5 seriously I needed to identify and remove the plank in my own eye before I could do anything about their splinter. That is what I have tried to do in this trilogy.

Books One and Two are my prayerful attempts at identifying the two critical planks which I believe seriously distort my vision and the vision of many other evangelical and charismatic leaders and congregations today. Book Three is my prescription for a course of treatment which might improve our vision, and so set us free to remove our brothers' splinters.

Whereas the *Ashburnham Insights* were written primarily for house-group leaders as hand-books for house-group study, *The death of Self* has been written especially for ministers, and I have primarily had a congregational application in mind. Of course I hope that these three books will also be widely used as a stimulating basis for a series of house-group meetings, but I particularly urge all in 'full-time Christian service' to work slowly through the trilogy, allowing the scorching light of Scripture to penetrate their presuppositions and experiences.

I am not a theologian. I am not even the full-time minister of a particular congregation. I'm just a man who has looked in his mirror and asked God to show him his planks. I have not attempted to construct watertight arguments to convince the staunchest doubter. Instead I've tried to pose questions which need careful thought; to propose omissions in our teaching; to point out imbalances in our emphases; and to plead that holy self-effacement and humble sacrifice may predominate in our personal, congregational and denominational lives.

I am sure that I must have got many things wrong. Even Paul admitted that his knowledge was imperfect. My problem is that I don't know what I'm wrong about; I doubt if I am the only person with this particular problem. Whilst I acknowledge it is unlikely that anybody will agree with everything in this trilogy, I do hope that everybody may be provoked and challenged by some part of each book.

Please read the books in the suggested order, and take care to look up all the Scripture references as you proceed through the text. Unless otherwise indicated, my biblical quotations are taken from the Jerusalem Bible.

My thanks go to all the members of both the Ashburnham Stable Family and the Ashburnham Parish Church for their unfailing patience, love and support. The following deserve special mention either for a contribution or for their company in a particularly formative experience: Ken Barham, Brian and Susan Betts, John and Marlis Bickersteth, Jean Breach, Teresa Clifton, Winifred Cox, David and Christine Freeland, Edmund Heddle, John Herbert, Sue Lindsay, Jo and Susie Marriott, Richard Martin, Margery May, Ralph May, Chris Nicholls, Jennifer Oldroyd, Alison Pain, David and Edna Parr, Catherine Rendall, and Roger and Penny Wilcock.

Timothy Pain

Crucify All Ambition

Passionately fierce the voice of God is pleading,
  Pleading with men to arm them for the fight;
See how those hands, majestically bleeding,
  Call us to rout the armies of the night.

Not to the work of sordid selfish saving
  Of our own souls to dwell with Him on high,
But to the soldier's splendid selfless braving,
  Eager to fight for Righteousness and die.

Peace does not mean the end of all our striving,
  Joy does not mean the drying of our tears;
Peace is the power that comes to souls arriving
  Up to the light where God himself appears.

Joy is the wine that God is ever pouring
  Into the hearts of those who strive with Him,
Light'ning their eyes to vision and adoring,
  Strength'ning their arms to warfare glad and grim.

So would I live and not in idle resting,
  Stupid as swine that wallow in the mire;
Fain would I fight, and be for ever breasting
  Danger and death for ever under fire.

Bread of Thy Body give me for my fighting,
  Give me to drink Thy Sacred Blood for wine,
While there are wrongs that need me for the righting,
  While there is warfare splendid and divine.

Give me, for light, the sunshine of Thy sorrow,
  Give me, for shelter, shadow of Thy Cross;
Give me to share the glory of Thy morrow,
  Gone from my heart the bitterness of Loss.

A short extract from *The Suffering God*
G A Studdert Kennedy

The Opening Sin

The crisis of self-surrender has always been, and must always be, regarded as the vital turning point of the religious life.

William James

The first sentence of a new book is often the hardest to write; great care has to be taken because it sets the tone for the whole volume. In fact, the first of anything is nearly always crucial. The first step, the first word, the first day at school, the first kiss, the birth of a first child; all of these are momentous events simply because they are the first. The second and third steps taken by a child are less faltering; the fourth and fifth words are spoken more fluently; a teenager's sixth and seventh kisses are much more fulfilling, and so on. Yet despite this, it is always the first event which is especially celebrated; it is the first that sets a precedent, provides a lasting memory, and points the direction for all future similar activities.

I believe that there are two reasons why the opening event in any series is so important. Firstly, it is because the original action in a sequence is usually the most difficult: later actions are normally performed with greater ease. Yuri Gagarin and Neil Armstrong are remembered because one was the first man in space and the other was the first man to set foot on the moon, but few people can name many of those astronauts who have followed them. Pioneers are admired and applauded because they face unknown dangers; those who come later follow in the relative safety of their predecessor's footsteps.

The second reason why the first in a series of events is so important is because it commonly marks an irreversible transfer from one stage to another. Virginity cannot be recovered once it has been lost. Knowledge cannot be unlearnt after it has been acquired: ever since the moment when the atom was first split mankind has been unable to return to the pre-nuclear age.

People long, both for themselves and for those dear to them, to achieve the next 'first' so that they can move on to another new stage. Yet when this has been reached many hanker after the stage they have passed. Most appreciate the benefits of nuclear and space technology, yet fear for their future and long for the simplicity of the 'good old days'. Mothers urge their babies on to walk and talk; then when the movement and noise begin they frequently yearn for the baby who is no more. Many people live in this tension, pulled by the conflicting emotions of nostalgia and curiosity.

No first has had a greater effect on mankind than the opening sin. We compare beautiful moments and places with Eden. We wonder what Eden could have been like. Even if we think of Paradise as parabolic it is surely partly because we know that mere words are inadequate to describe accurately the beauty and emotions hinted at in the first three chapters of Genesis.

We read about Eve's sin and wonder what might have happened if she had resisted the serpent's attack. We speak of that moment when Adam and Eve were ejected from the Garden in disgrace, and call it 'the Fall'. But we forget that the very first sin was not committed by Eve. The time when her teeth sank deep into the forbidden fruit was not the moment which inaugurated the new era of darkness in God's creation. Sin had already begun.

And it began in an even more perfect place than Eden: for the very first sin was committed in the highest and holiest place by a being whose beauty and glory have only once been surpassed in the history of all creation.

Surprisingly, the story of the opening sin is not found in Genesis. Instead, it is recorded in Isaiah 14 and Ezekiel 28. These two chapters are critical for any understanding about sin, because the very first sin set a precedent for all future sin, dictated the path that sin would take throughout Scripture, and provided the pattern for sin which is still imitated today. If we are people who consider ourselves to be dead to sin in our lives and to be opposed to sin in the world, then we need both to grasp the implications of the opening sin, and, even more importantly, to be intransigently opposed to the presence of this particular sin today.

The first ten verses of Ezekiel 28 describe the ruler of Tyre and contain a prophetic message for him. However, the tone of the chapter changes from verse 11 onwards. There Ezekiel describes not the ruler or prince of Tyre, but the king of Tyre; and pours out a lamentation over him. The words used about the ruler in verses 1–10 are appropriate for a human being; and in verse 2 Ezekiel reminds the ruler that he is a man and not a God. But the description of the king in verses 12 and 13 is highly inappropriate for any mortal. Surely these words can only be applied to Satan himself: 'You were once an exemplar of perfection, full of wisdom, perfect in beauty; you were in Eden, in the garden of God.'

After his creation Satan was intimate with God. He lived on the holy mountain of God. He had been provided with a guardian cherub. He was blameless in all his ways, splendid in wisdom, skilful in operation, perfect in beauty: the supreme example of perfection in God's creation. Verse 15 states, 'Your behaviour was exemplary from the day of your creation until the day when evil was first found in you.' But what was that evil? What form did the violence and sin of verse 16 take? Ezekiel 28 may reveal the original sinner, but it is Isaiah 14 which unveils the original sin.

As with Ezekiel 28, the first part of Isaiah 14 begins with a satire on a human king—this time the king of Babylon. But from verse 10 onwards another, altogether more sinister, figure can be seen behind the earthly king. Again, surely these words can only have been written about Satan: 'Your magnificence has been flung down to Sheol with the music of your harps; underneath you a bed of maggots, and over you a blanket of worms. How did you come to fall from the heavens, Daystar, son of Dawn?'

Well, how did this magnificent creature come to fall? What did he do that was so terrible? What was the deed that transferred creation from light to darkness and from perfection to impurity? What form did the action take that set the precedent for all future wrongdoing? What was the opening sin?

Isaiah's taunt in verses 13–14 makes the sin quite plain, 'You who used to think to yourself, "I will climb up to the heavens; and higher than the stars of God I will set my throne. I will sit on the Mount of Assembly in the recesses of the north. I will climb to the top of thunderclouds, I will rival the Most High."' This fivefold 'I will' which came from the lips of Satan, this was the opening sin. Ambition, naked ambition, was the very first evil to pollute God's creation. Satan's ambition for advancement was the stain which discoloured heaven, maybe even before the dawn of time. Ambition is the source of all mankind's wrong thoughts and foul deeds. Ambition: this must be recognised as the father of all sin.

Most people do not realise this. Nearly all commentators identify pride as the sin which caused Lucifer's ejection from heaven, quoting Proverbs 29:23 as support for their opinion; but Satan's ambition preceded his pride. It usually does. Pride is a smug and arrogant contentment either with oneself, one's position, or one's attainments; whereas ambition is a devilish discontentment with these things. Both feelings ignore God and neglect or refuse to give him thanks for his provision. Ambition may, as in Satan's case, lead on to pride, though it may also result in either disappointment or despair. But pride normally only fans the pre-existent flames of ambition.

Satan was not proud of his throne's position; the opposite is true, he was dissatisfied with his seat below God. Satan was not proud of being God's second in command; instead he was discontented with only being number two in the heavenly hierarchy. The truth is that Satan wanted to usurp God. He was ambitious to become God, and so tried to depose him. That is why he fell. And the cause of his fall then became his principal weapon in the war of attrition which he has unceasingly waged against mankind ever since he was ejected from heaven.

This first volume in *The death of Self* trilogy is my attempt to trace the use of that weapon throughout Scripture; to note its demonic development; to observe the divine reaction; to study Christ's battle with, and teaching on, ambition; to name it as the main plank in the eye of the present-day evangelical and charismatic church; and to make some tentative suggestions about the church's attitude to this sin today. For I believe that ambition is not only the opening sin, but is also the unrecognised sin; and that it remains Satan's primary weapon in his ongoing attempts to deceive, and to destroy God's kingdom.

We live at a time when it is fashionable to consider ambition a virtue, so I urge all readers to put aside any personal presuppositions about this topic. We must only allow Scripture to determine our thinking and interpret our experience. My prayer is that all my readers will be intellectually stretched and spiritually blessed as they consider what the Bible says about ambition. And that then they will have the courage daily to incorporate their conclusions into their personal and congregational lives, and, if they are preachers, into their teaching.

Ambition in Eden

Let it be remembered, then, that sin is a unit and always and necessarily consists in selfish ultimate intention and in nothing else. This intention is sin, and every phase of sin resolves itself into selfishness.

Charles Finney

Nobody can begin to imagine accurately the depths of intimacy and mutual delight enjoyed by God and man in Eden. Genesis 2 presents an image of absolute contentment. God is seen fashioning man, breathing life into him, planting a beautiful garden, and placing man in that same garden. Man is shown creatively naming the animals, cultivating the garden, and exclaiming with joy at God's gift to him of woman.

But this idyllic picture of satisfaction and enjoyment was disrupted by the one who had been ejected from heaven because of his ambition. He who had been discontented with his own heavenly lot attempted to spread sedition on earth with his suggestion to Eve that she should think about improving her own situation. Satan, in the disguise of the serpent, states in Genesis 3:5, 'On the day you eat it your eyes will be opened and you will be like gods, knowing good and evil.' He was appealing to Eve to want to be different, to be ambitious for a fresh experience, and to stretch out her hand and clasp to herself the knowledge which God had reserved for himself alone.

The forbidden fruit of the tree of the knowledge of good and evil clearly does not symbolise omniscience, as post-Eve man has never possessed infinite knowledge.

Nor can the fruit represent some sort of ability to discriminate morally, for the story of Eden would be a nonsense if the garden-dwellers did not already possess this freedom: surely God's prohibition and Satan's temptation presuppose that unfallen man could already choose whether or not to obey God. Rather, the essence of the temptation was the suggestion that Eve should herself sample the experience of deciding what was good or evil, and of acting in accordance with her own opinion, irrespective of God's thoughts on the matter.

I believe that when Eve succumbed to Satan's temptation to be ambitious for forbidden knowledge and a new experience, she was both claiming moral independence of God and refusing to continue to acknowledge her status as a created being. Her desire for, and then her acquisition of, this knowledge was an explicit denial of God's revealed will. And to this day ambition always remains a direct attack on the sovereignty of God.

The ambitious thoughts which Satan whispered in the woman's ear were not in themselves the cause of God's punishment. Eve did not fall until she had yielded her will to these thoughts, and had chosen to form her own opinion in defiance of God's word; she then decided to act upon her sinful mental intention. Satan was not ejected from heaven for wishing that he had been stationed even higher, but for declaring five times, *I will* be number one. Ambition is not a childish day-dream about scoring a hat-trick at Wembley or a century at Lords. Ambition only begins when desire develops into intention; when planning changes into presumption; when the words 'I will' are formed in a human mind; whenever a man or woman thinks or acts independently of God's will.

Genesis 3 suggests several consequences of Eve's ambition, all of which are relevant to the church today. Her ambition affected and involved others. It always does. Verse 6 states, 'She gave some also to her husband who was with her, and he ate it.' Her husband, her children, in fact all her descendants, were damaged in some way by her deed. It was the same with Satan. Some commentators suggest that Revelation 12:4 indicates that a third of all angels shared in Satan's ejection from heaven; certainly Revelation 12:9 implies that he did not leave alone.

Then Eve's ambition caused her to feel shame. Verse 7 records, 'The eyes of both of them were opened and they realised that they were naked. So they sewed fig-leaves together to make themselves loin-cloths.' It is interesting that they were not embarassed by their ambition or disobedience, but by their thoroughly natural nakedness. The fig-leaf episode has nothing to do with sexuality; it is merely another way of demonstrating discontentment with their God-given condition. Having tasted the fruit of moral independence, Adam and Eve audaciously attempted to improve on God's provision for their lives.

It is still the same today. We live in an age when Satan has convinced both the world and the church that ambition is not a vice but a virtue. Like those first garden-dwellers, few are ashamed of their ambitions. But when human ambitions have been realised there is often still an element of shame about any remaining evidence of the pre-successful state. Many eminent people end up embarrassed not by their success or its price, but by their parents, spouse or past, and, like Adam and Eve, will do anything to cover up their humble origins.

Another result of Eve's ambition was that both she and Adam felt a need to conceal themselves from God. Verse 8 suggests that they tried to hide among the trees of the garden, and shows clearly that if God seems distant it is man who has moved. When God was searching for them they answered with a strange reply. In verse 10 Adam says, 'I was afraid because I was naked, so I hid.'

I think that any ambition means that God himself is, to the extent of that ambition, less desirable. So Adam and Eve's ambition for knowledge meant that friendship and fellowship with their Creator were that much less attractive: new interests had taken their time and attention. I find few things as embarrassing as bumping into an old friend whom I have neglected because of a new concern. I too would rather hide and hope that I am not noticed.

But why were Adam and Eve afraid? Why, when they heard God calling, did they not take off their fig-leaves, hide them, and pretend that they were still naked? They knew God was used to their nakedness, so why were they frightened of being seen by him with nothing on? And, most puzzling of all, why were they not in the slightest bit frightened of being seen wearing fig-leaves?

Any ambition is always a distraction from God himself; and I suggest that they were so preoccupied with their new experience that they had forgotten their old friend the Maker. Perhaps their shame at their pre-fallen state was so overpowering that in their distraction they naively presumed God would be equally embarrassed by their nakedness. Certainly when I am preoccupied with a new idea I tend to presume that any sane person will be equally fascinated, especially if the person has been closely involved with me in my previous interest. When they hid among the trees Adam and Eve were not attempting to deceive God but thought they were doing him a favour. The only satisfactory explanation for their fear is that they had been so deceived that they actually thought God would be delighted by the fig-leaves.

The outcome of their ambition was that, no longer knowing God intimately, they had unconsciously altered their understanding of his thoughts. They were not attempting to deceive God, but to please him. And still today many friends of God sincerely, but mistakenly, believe that the results of their ambitions please God. They are as wrong as Adam and Eve were.

Another consequence of the first human sin was Adam's inability to admit that he was wrong. In verse 11 God asks him, 'Have you been eating of the tree I forbade you to eat?' And in the following verse Adam prevaricates with, 'It was the woman you put with me...' When Eve was questioned by God she also would not, or could not, accept responsibility; in verse 13 she says, 'The serpent tempted me...' Both Adam and Eve were factually correct in what they said. It was the woman, whom God had placed with the man, who had handed him the fruit; and the serpent had tempted her to eat. But God had not asked them why they had eaten, simply whether or not they had eaten.

And so today circumstances pressurise us to be ambitious. Society expects and encourages ambition. We strive for promotion, improvement, and a better standard of living. We teach our children independence. Yet when God puts his finger on me I squeal like Adam and Eve and blame my circumstances; I blame the devil; I even, sometimes, blame God himself. It is still as hard as it was in Eden to admit to God that ambition is sin, and that we have committed this, the original and most terrible sin.

The final outcome of the first human sin was divine judgement. Spiritual death came first, quickly followed by separation from their Maker. The serpent, the woman, and then the man were cursed and expelled from Eden. The pair had declared themselves to be the arbiters of good and evil, and so God intervened to prevent them from taking the inevitable next step along the path of ambition, which would have been to lay claim to immortality. Cherubs, armed with the flame of a flashing sword, were posted as sentries to guard the way to the tree of life.

Ambition was earth's, as well as heaven's, opening sin. It provided the pattern and precedent for evil; it dictated the direction which all sin has taken since Eden; and God remains implacably opposed to it. For ambition strikes at his sovereignty, usurps his authority, and separates him from his children. Judgement is his only possible reaction.

And yet Genesis 3:21 records God taking a most surprising action. Instead of stripping the rebels of their fig-leaves he generously offers them a permanent garment made from skins. Judgement is wrapped in grace and love. The pair recognise that God's provision is better than human accomplishment, discard their leaves, and dress themselves in God's gracious gift. Maybe they learnt from this that God's provision is always superior to any man-made effort. But mankind has certainly not taken note, for down through the centuries the pattern of ambition, judgement and grace has gone on repeating itself, waiting for one to come who could break the cycle by crucifying his ambition, and so offer mankind freedom from its self-imposed misery.

Ambition Takes Control

Let death be to you the most desirable thing on earth; death to self, and fellowship with Christ. Surely one ought to say, "Anything to bring me to death, for a life of full fellowship with God and Christ". Oh! come and cast this self-life at the feet of Jesus.

Andrew Murray

Ambition, like Satan, comes in many disguises, and it is important to recognise these for what they are. We are quick to denounce greed as sin, but slow to realise that it is a sub-section or facet of ambition; for the word 'greed' is merely shorthand for the longer phrase 'ambition for wealth or food'. There is little disagreement with the proposition that lust is sinful, but once again it must be appreciated that the word 'lust' is only an abbreviation of the expression 'ambition for sexual indulgence'. In fact, all of the seven so-called deadly, or capital, sins are either aspects or results of ambition.

Yet despite this, most people believe that though some forms of ambition may be wrong, ambition itself is either good or morally neutral. Other people suggest that pride, envy, lust, gluttony, avarice, sloth and so on, are demonic distortions of ambition rather than unsullied ambition itself. And some people state that it depends upon the nature of the objects of the ambition. Either way, a widespread feeling exists today that an area or object of ambition must exist which is not sinful.

But as some of the Old Testament material on this topic is examined we will note that God repeatedly reserves his harshest judgements for those who are ambitious, irrespective of the form or object of their ambition, and that he continually attempts to create a society and people where ambition is either irrelevant or as difficult as is divinely possible without restricting man's free will.

Of course much depends on our understanding of the word 'ambition'. No doubt some will argue that an ambition to live without sin could never be wrong, but those who say this fail to distinguish between ambition and desire. This is a much-needed and important distinction.

Ambition has its roots in discontentment. Discontentment is not necessarily sinful in itself, but it is dangerous because it is fertile soil for the seed of ambition. Ambition does not begin until desire moves into intention; until a man or woman thinks 'I will'; until there is an element of presumption. And I think that it is this presumption which is the sinful nucleus in the cell of ambition.

All believers should be discontented with their sin all believers should earnestly desire to live without sin, but any believer who thinks that he will live without sinning presumes too much, and has succumbed to the sin of ambition.

Everybody knows that all Christians are meant to obey God as a response to God's love. But most people mistakenly assume that disobedience is the sole antithesis of obedience. It isn't. Disobedience and presumption are the twin antitheses of obedience. To disobey God is either to do something he has forbidden or not to do something he has commanded. To presume upon God is to do anything which he has not commanded. Both actions are equally sinful. Eve sinned when she ate the apple, and she sinned when she donned the fig leaf. The first action was disobedience, the second was presumptious. The emphasis in contemporary preaching would suggest that the Bible stresses the problem of disobedience. Yet, surprisingly, the Bible contains more about God's opposition to our presumption than about his sadness at our disobedience.

Satan presumed that he would be able to usurp God: if he had not thought it possible he would not have tried: his desire may have remained, but it would not have developed into a sinful action. Eve presumed either that God had lied when he said, 'on the day you eat of it you shall most surely die'; or she presumed that the acquisition of the forbidden knowledge would be worth the risk of whatever God meant by death. And Adam presumed that God would be pleased with his fig-leaves. Ambition only exists while a sinner presumes that the object of his ambition is attainable.

When Eve sinned she was sampling the experience of deciding for herself what was right and wrong: she presumed that she knew best. All ambition is based on the two false presumptions that, firstly, what God has already provided is inferior or inadequate; and that, secondly, what is sought will either remedy or improve this deficiency.

After the expulsion from Eden, the next act of divine judgement was the Great Deluge, related in Genesis 6–9. We are not concerned here with details of the Flood itself, but with the human activity which preceded and prompted it. Some commentators suggest that the strange references to the Nephilim, in Genesis 6:1–4, may contain the reason for the judgement of the Flood, and they identify the sons of God mentioned here with the angels referred to in Jude 6. But I do not think Jude 6 should be linked with Genesis 6:1–4 as the angels in Jude 6 will not be judged until the final day of judgement at the return of Christ.

If the great wickedness alluded to in Genesis 6:5 is the puzzling sexual alliance of the preceding four verses, it must be verse 2 which nails the sin. 'The sons of God, looking at the daughters of men, saw they were pleasing, so they married as many as they chose.' Their sin was not their natural desire for attractive girls, but their presumption, their ambition, their independent decision-making which meant that 'they married as many as *they* chose'.

When Jesus referred to the days before the deluge, in Matthew 24:37–38, he catalogued the evil which had precipitated the judgement: 'People were eating and drinking, marrying wives and husbands, right up to the day Noah went into the ark, and the Flood came and destroyed them all.'

These people were not condemned because they were ambitious for things which were evil: the Bible does not say that they were greedy drunkards who indulged in regular orgies. In fact, the objects of their ambition could hardly have been healthier. Instead, I think that the continuous evil imaginations of Genesis 6:6 refer to undiluted ambition. Their sin was that they presumed to do all of the thoroughly normal things referred to by Jesus without any reference to God. The consistent message of Scripture is that God is more angered by apathy than by antagonism; so these early men and women were condemned because they ignored God and ate whatever *they* wanted to eat, drank whatever *they* wanted to drink, and married whoever *they* chose. Their independent, presumptuous actions struck hard at the sovereignty of God; so judgement came—but a judgement which was wrapped in the grace of the ark, the guidance of the dove, and the glorious promise of the rainbow.

And so the pattern goes on throughout the Old Testament. Genesis 11:1–9 tells the story of the confusion of languages and scattering of people at Babel. Why? Because of their three-fold ambition: 'Come, let us make bricks and bake them in the fire'; 'Let us build ourselves a town and a tower with its top reaching heaven'; and 'Let us make a name for ourselves'. They achieved two of their ambitions; they made the bricks and built the tower, but God intervened to prevent completion of the town. Once again, the objects of their ambitions appear harmless to our deceived contemporary eyes: one of my best friends is a brick-maker! But the problem was that they were discontented with God's provision for them and sought to improve on it without any reference to him. They wanted to achieve something. They wanted to reach heaven by their own efforts. They wanted to provide for themselves. They craved recognition and a lasting memorial. So God judged them because their ambition meant that they were ignoring him.

In Genesis 12:2; 12:7; and again in 13:15–17 God promised Abram children. Nearly ten years after the original promise Abram pointed out to God, in Genesis 15:2–6, that he was still childless, so God confirmed that Abram would definitely have an heir. But despite God's promise of provision Abram and Sarai presumed that they should take the matter into their own hands. Abram said 'I will' to Sarai's plan, and Genesis 16 relates the first sorry instalment in the Ishmael saga. Fourteen years later Isaac was born to the renamed Abraham and Sarah, and Abraham began to understand the difference between a promise and a command. It is a lesson which many need to learn today. When God says he will do something he is not asking us to do anything—other than to remain loyal, faithful and patient.

Nobody in the Old Testament knew God better than Moses. His impetuous ambition to right wrongs had been burned out of him by forty years as a hired shepherd in the Midian wilderness. His famous meekness meant that he needed his elder brother to speak on his behalf. Through the plagues, the crossing of the Red Sea, the manna, quails and everlasting sandals he knew that God's provision could not be improved. He was content. But in Numbers 20 he was ensnared. When the people opposed and challenged him because of the absence of water, Moses went to God for instructions and was told 'Take the branch and call the community together, you and your brother Aaron. Then, in full view of them, order this rock to give water' (Num 20:8). But instead of speaking to the rock once, Moses struck it twice: he presumed that he knew better than God.

Maybe Moses thought he had misheard God; maybe he thought God had made a mistake; perhaps in the heat of the moment he got carried away. But I suspect that he was relying on experience rather than fresh instructions. Many years before a similar situation had arisen, and in Exodus 17 we read that God had then instructed Moses to strike a rock to provide water. In fact, nearly all the miracles that God had worked through Moses had depended upon the right use of his staff; this was the first time in his long life of service that God had told him to use words of authority. And many people today are so set in patterns of work, life and ministry that they are unable either to recognise or to obey new directions from God. Like Moses, they presume. And, like Moses, they can appear successful. Water gushed from the twice-struck rock; but in God's service the end never justifies the means, and God judged Moses' presumption saying, in Numbers 20:12, 'You shall not lead this assembly into the land I am giving them.'

Right through the Old Testament God ruthlessly punished ambition and presumption. Joshua 7 tells how Achan's ambition to possess a robe meant that he forfeited his life and the Israelites lost the battle of Ai. The sad episode, in Judges 14, of Samson's ambition for a Philistine wife and the loss of her to his best man after only a week of marriage was not enough to teach him to be content. Twenty years later he fell in love with another Philistine woman and suffered the terrible consequences recorded in Judges 16.

The people of Israel became discontented with being governed by judges, they wanted to be like other nations and be ruled by a king. In 1 Samuel 8:10–18 Samuel explained the disadvantages of a monarchy, but the people refused to listen. God told Samuel, in 1 Samuel 8:7, that this ambition meant, 'They have rejected me from ruling over them.' And what a fine mess the kings made!

Saul had only been king for a short while when he was rejected by God for betraying the trust put in him. What had he done that was so wrong? Firstly, Saul was so worried when Samuel was late arriving to offer sacrifice before battle that he presumed to offer the sacrifice himself (1 Sam 13:7–15). Then, secondly, after the battle against the Amalekites, Saul kept back the best of the sheep, cattle and all that was good instead of destroying it. In his greed, he presumed that he had the right to interpret God's instructions (1 Sam 15:7–23).

The words of Samuel in 1 Samuel 15:23 point out the

parallel nature of disobedience and presumption, and they also provide an awesome reminder of God's attitude to ambition and presumption. 'Rebellion is a sin of sorcery, presumption a crime of teraphim.' To God, presumption is no different from obtaining guidance from an occult source. (The mention of teraphim refers to the practice of consulting the tutelary idols of houses and property.) We would do well to remember this principle today.

David's ambition for Bathsheba, 2 Samuel 11, is well known; so too is his punishment, 2 Samuel 12:13–23, where once again judgement is wrapped in grace: Solomon—David and Bathsheba's second child—is chosen by God as David's heir in preference to other, better qualified, sons.

But David's presumption in ordering a census in 1 Chronicles 21, appears to have been even more reprehensible to God than his adultery and murder, though to many modern eyes the latter is much worse than the former. Moses' census in Numbers 1:1–2 had not attracted divine censure, so why did 70,000 men have to die of pestilence when David took a census? The answer is simple. God had told Moses to do it, whereas David only thought that it was the sensible thing to do: he had presumed.

Space does not permit the listing of every sin of ambition and presumption mentioned in the Old Testament. Those interested will make the time to delve through the Scriptures themselves. But the incidents that have been mentioned should provide convincing proof that God loathes ambition, hates presumption, and is repulsed by any action which is not initiated by him alone.

Ambition Attacked

Forbid it, Lord, that I should boast
Save in the cross of Christ my God;
The very things that charm me most—
I sacrifice them to His blood.

Isaac Watts

The Old Testament not only lists God's reactions to man's ambition, it also records God's provisions for the prevention of human ambition. The Bible presents Yahweh, the God of Israel, as the great giver, and not as an automatic rewarder. In fact his first words to man, in Genesis 1:29, were, 'See, I give you all . . .' At times his giving may depend upon the fulfilment of certain conditions, but this does not mean that any one who meets those conditions will definitely receive a particular gift. God gives what he chooses, when he chooses, to whom he chooses, and sometimes he selects very—to human eyes—undeserving causes.

The names of God reveal the nature of God, and one of the most common names is *El Shaddai*. Many render this as Almighty God, but the masculine and military connotations of the word almighty are suggested more by the name *Yahweh Sabaoth* (the Lord God of hosts or armies) than by *El Shaddai*. This name can be translated as either the Mountain God or the Big Breasted God. If these two possibilities are taken together the maternal nature of a God of 'mountainous' provision becomes clear. God loves to provide for his children, and he wants his sons and daughters to depend upon his provision: to be breast fed, not bottle fed!

In Exodus 3:14, we read that the special name of God, which he revealed to Moses at the burning bush, is *Yahweh*. This is an archaic form of the verb 'to be' and is most commonly understood to mean 'I Am what I Am'. But it can be rendered with equal accuracy as 'I Will what I Will'. If God abhors the ambitious 'I will's' of his creatures, he delights to say 'I will' to his children. He is the great 'I Will', and he longs for his people to depend on his promises. A Jew could be executed for daring to utter this name of God, and I suggest that we should exercise great caution before we ever say 'I will'.

Many say that to reject ambition means to encourage passivity. I am not sure what is so terrible about passivity, but it is not the only possible alternative to ambition. Irresponsible inactivity is not a synonym for trusting in God's provision and God's promises. God gave Eden to Adam, but Adam had to take care of it. God gave Adam fruit to eat, but he had to cultivate it. God gave Noah detailed instructions for the Ark, but Noah had to build it. God gave the centenarian Abraham the promise of a son, but Abraham and Sarah had to copulate. God gave manna to the Israelites in the desert, but they had to gather exactly the right amount, and demonstrate their dependence by not keeping any for the following day—except on Fridays. God gave his people a land flowing with milk and honey, but they had to fight every inch of the way to possess it.

In every case the initiative came from God. He freely gave property, prominence, prowess, or promises to whoever he chose; but the recipient of his choice had to be an effective steward of the gift—whether it was resources, responsibility, or ability. The ambitious person asks himself, 'Where shall I go? What do I want?

What shall I do?' But the child of God asks his Father, 'Where have you placed me? What have you given me? How do I steward this?'

The principle of absolute reliance upon God's provision is underlined in the Old Testament battles. Exodus 14 describes the first attack upon the people of Israel, when the Egyptian army chased the escaping Israelites to the edge of the Sea of Reeds. In verses 13–14 Moses answered the terrified people's cries: 'Have no fear! Stand firm, and you will see what Yahweh will do to save you today: the Egyptians you see today, you will never see again. Yahweh will do the fighting for you: you have only to keep still.' On the following day the Israelites were given a stunning demonstration of Yahweh Sabaoth's power as he drove home the point that he does not need our help in the provision of victory.

The first battle that the Israelites fought is recorded in Exodus 17:8–16. This time the people had to do the fighting, and some of them were killed. But again Moses' outstretched arms showed that victory depended on God. The lesson was repeated at the battle of Jericho (Joshua 6). The people had the responsibility of becoming skilled fighters, but they had to know that success depended on God's provision of victory rather than on their discipline and ability. At the end of Joshua's long life he said, in Joshua 23:3, 'Yahweh your God himself has fought for you', and in verse 5, 'Yahweh your God will himself drive them out before you; he will cast them out before you and you will take possession of their country as Yahweh your God promised you.'

At the outset of his career Gideon had to learn, as we see in Judges 7, that victory depended not on numerical supremacy, but on divine intervention. Mighty, conquering David began his military life by appreciating that victory was not determined by superior equipment. In 1 Samuel 17:47 we read that he told Goliath, 'all this assembly may know that it is not by sword or by spear that Yahweh gives the victory, for Yahweh is lord of the battle and he will deliver you into our power'.

God's antipathy to ambition extended to establishing a system which made personal advancement impossible. The tribal system determined in which part of Canaan any individual lived. The hereditary system of office meant that only Aaron's direct descendants could be priests, and they could not be anything else. A descendant of Reuben might have thought that he would make an excellent priest, but such ambition was out of the question as the office was unattainable. It was the same with the Levites. Unless you were related to Levi you could not serve as an attendant in the Temple. God had created a religious structure which made ambition well nigh impossible.

It was different with the judges. This was not a hereditary office, in fact when the elderly Samuel wrongly appointed his two sons as judges (1 Samuel 8:1), the people demanded a king and the office came to an end. Judges were not elected by the people, nor were they self-appointed; it did not matter who their father was or what their sex was. A man or woman could only become a judge over Israel when God raised them up. Judges 2:16 states, 'Then Yahweh appointed judges for them.' God did this by choosing a particular person, and then making his choice plain by giving that person the gift of his Spirit. The first judge was Othniel. Judges 3:10 states, 'The Spirit of Yahweh came on him; he became judge in Israel and set out to fight. Yahweh delivered the king of

Edom, Cushan-rishathaim, into his hands.' The same gift of the Spirit was given to Gideon, Judges 6:34; to Jephthah, Judges 11:29; and to Samson, Judges 13:25; 14:6, 19. Anybody could desire that God would choose him, but nobody could be ambitious for the office, for the matter was entirely out of human control.

What applied to the judges was also true of the prophets: God chose them, then showed that he had chosen them by giving them his Spirit. No one could aspire to the office, and no one could reject it. They might go astray and betray their choice by becoming a false prophet or a corrupt judge, but they could not stop being a prophet or a judge. Isaiah 6; Jeremiah 1:4–19; Ezekiel 3; Hosea 1:2; Amos 7:14–15 and Jonah 1:1 are accounts of a prophet being called by God.

When God allowed the Israelites to have a king he did not permit the people to choose the king. There was to be no ambitious jockeying for position, no attempt to influence people, no electioneering. Instead, God personally selected Saul. God pointed Saul out to Samuel, 1 Samuel 9:17; Samuel anointed Saul, 10:1; God gave Saul the gift of his Spirit, 10:10; and the choice was dramatically confirmed when Saul was chosen by lot, 10:21.

It was the same with David. When God rejected Saul because of his presumption it was God himself who selected the successor. He pointed David out to Samuel, 1 Samuel 16:12; Samuel publicly anointed him, 16:13; and God immediately confirmed his choice: 'And the Spirit of Yahweh seized on David and stayed with him from that day on' (16:13).

God also created a financial structure for his chosen people which made ambition as difficult as was possible without turning people into puppets. In Exodus 21:1–11 God sets out his laws concerning slaves: they had to be given the option of freedom after six years. Exodus 22:25 forbids usury: 'If you lend money to any one of my people, to any poor man among you, you must not play the usurer with him: you must not demand interest from him.' Exodus 23:10–11 orders a fallow year for food production in every seventh year, so that the poor can take food from the land. To appreciate God's thoroughness in inaugurating a financial system which was both equitable and practical look carefully at the detailed legislation in Leviticus 25. Verses 20–22 answer to all those who suppose it is completely impractical to talk of crucifying ambition: these verses can be applied ad infinitum.

God's system of the sabbatical year, the jubilee year and the redemption of property, loans and enfranchisement was designed to encourage men to depend totally on his provision, and to ensure that they were careful stewards of that provision. His system was meant to liberate his people from the sin of ambition. But men preferred their own presumption. God's laws were first ignored, then forgotten. The opening sin gradually established an effective stranglehold on God's people. Ambition—personal, tribal and national—quickly became rife. The world, though it did not realise it, was still waiting for one to come who would resist the temptations of ambition and presumption, who would depend absolutely on God's provision, who would crucify ambition, and who would call others to take up their crosses and follow him down the path of contentment and self-denial.

Ambition Overcome

When Christ calls a man, he bids him come and die.

Dietrich Bonhoeffer

Two facts can be anticipated if my suggestion is correct that ambition is the first and most terrible of sins. Firstly, that Satan will attack Jesus in this area. And secondly, that no ambition or presumption will ever be found in Jesus' life. Ambition is unlikely to be Satan's principal weapon if he does not bother to use it against Jesus. And it cannot be a sin, let alone the most terrible of sins, if a speck of ambition or presumption can be detected in the life of Jesus.

Philippians 2:6–8 declares: 'His state was divine, yet he did not cling to his equality with God but emptied himself to assume the condition of a slave, and became as men are; and being as all men are, he was humbler yet, even to accepting death, death on a cross.' From before the beginning Jesus was God. He possessed all the attributes that express the essential nature of God: all the divine prerogatives were his by right. Yet he surrendered the public honour due to him as God.

The one thing he could not give up was his divine nature, but he gave up everything else. In particular, he gave up the glory to which his divine nature entitled him, and which he had enjoyed before the Incarnation. If he had not given up his glory, it would always have been visible in his human body—as it was at the Transfiguration—and his divine nature would have been obvious to all. Even the reflected glory on Moses' face was so blinding that he had to cover his face (Exodus 33–34).

The New International Version renders verse 7, 'but made himself nothing...' It is amazing that the great 'I Will what I Will' should relinquish his glory, make himself nothing, take the form of a human slave, live a life of submission and humble obedience, and share all the weaknesses of the human condition—except sin.

When God became man that meant embracing the indignity of infant incontinence, impotence and ignorance. The one who had brought the universe into being with a word lay in an animal feeding trough unable to reason, remember or pray. As the child matured he experienced the poverty and bewilderment of a refugee, then the limitations and anonymity of life in an occupied town, in a part of the country that was despised by educated Jews from the South. He worked with his hands, gradually realising who he was and who he had been. But he told no one. And nobody guessed. He looked set for a life of obscurity and irrelevance.

For over thirty years the Son was the perfect demonstration of a life lived in absolute contentment with the Father's provision. God had placed him in Nazareth and had given him the twin tasks of carpentry and caring for his widowed mother. He had no ambition to better himself or improve his domestic circumstances. He simply lived one day at a time, always depending only on his Father for direction and instruction.

Then when he was 'about thirty' (Luke 3:23)—and to most people, too old to start anything new—there came a day which was different. He put down his tools, left his family, and went to the river Jordan to be baptised by cousin John. Matthew 3:13–17; Mark 1:9–11; and Luke 3:21–22 supply the details, and the Father provided the instructions. Then Mark 1:12 relates that, 'Immediately afterwards the Spirit drove him out into the wilderness.'

Luke 4:1–3 shows that the Devil tempted Jesus in the wilderness for forty long days, and that during this time he ate nothing. Luke does not imply that the three temptations recorded in detail were the totality of the temptation, rather that they were the climax of the temptation. Luke seems to suggest that Satan had been building up to these three temptations for nearly six weeks. They were to be his knock-out blows. Both Matthew and Luke record the same three temptations, though in a different order.

First, a very hungry Jesus was pressed to tell some stones to turn into loaves. The principle behind the temptation leapt straight from Eden. Jesus was meant, first, to be discontented with God's direction and provision; and, second, to attempt personally to improve on that provision. Most commentators suggest that this was a temptation to disobey; but God had not forbidden Jesus to turn stones into bread, so he would not have been disobedient if he had done so. No, the temptation was not to disobedience, but to presumption. Jesus was being tempted to do something which God had not suggested; to act independently of God; to work a miracle without any instructions; to move from a thoroughly healthy and natural desire for food to a sinful presumption to satisfy that desire.

Secondly, according to Matthew, Satan tempted Jesus to throw himself off the Temple parapet, trusting in angels to preserve him. Perhaps Satan hoped that Jesus would die prematurely, but more probably this was another attempt to make Jesus be ambitious for danger, for prominence, for a thrilling new supernatural experience; and once again he pressed Jesus to presume to act without any divine instructions. But Jesus resisted the temptation.

Thirdly, Jesus was tempted to be ambitious for power, prestige and influence. This time disobedience was a distinct possibility because God had sent Jesus to be a suffering servant, not a mighty king. Satan did not only want Jesus to worship him, that was just the means to an end. Satan wanted Jesus to commit the very first sin. He wanted Jesus to act independently of God, to presume he knew better than God, to be dissatisfied with his life of anonymity, and to thirst for prestige, power, and public acclamation. But Jesus rejected the seductive attraction of ambition. He did not sin.

In these temptations, Jesus was not tempted to perform evil deeds, but to do his own deeds. However, Jesus never did anything on his own initiative: he only did those few things which the Father told him. It is striking that God later freely gave Jesus all the objects of ambition which had been offered to him by Satan. He turned five rolls into enough bread to satisfy 5,000 hungry men; he was miraculously preserved from death when, on a stormy night, he walked across deep water; and God gave him all power, all glory, all authority, and the title King of kings.

John 5:19, 30; 6:38; 7:28–29; 8:26, 28–29; 10:18; and 12:49–50 are an extraordinary series of sayings which must be taken at face value. Jesus, the perfect man, the one all Christians are called to follow, the great healer, the mighty deliverer, the wonder counsellor, was the man who stated time and again that he himself could do nothing. How many of his followers today can say the same about themselves? How many even desire to say the same? How many, if they did say the same, would be given corrective counselling by their minister? But Jesus, by a titanic effort of self-denial, restricted himself to saying, doing and going what and where the Father told him. He came from heaven as both the incarnation of God and the perfect example of a man made in the divine image. This meant that he came not to do his own will, but to do the will of the one who sent him. Ambition was out of the question.

He never made this clearer than on the Mount of Olives. Luke 22:39–46 tells the story of the supreme moment of temptation in the life of Jesus: a struggle not with Satan but with God. The issue to be decided was whose will would be implemented, the Son's or the Father's?

The first half of verse 42 suggests that Jesus, confronted with the cup of God's wrath against mankind (with which he had totally identified himself), earnestly longed not to have to endure the cross. At that moment Jesus shared the human desire for forgiveness without the cross and for grace without righteous judgement.

The second part of verse 42 must be the climax of the entire Bible, perhaps the most important moment in human history. Jesus could not manage to align himself with God's will, but he could submit to it, so he said, 'Nevertheless, let your will be done, not mine.' Here we see the antithesis of ambition and presumption. Here the die was cast, the real struggle was over, and Jesus could go through the voluntary agonies of the next twelve hours with amazing equanimity.

In the three brief years of notoriety following his long

years of obscurity Jesus provided his followers with the example of ambition defeated, and with teaching on a positive way forward. Just as the Father had sought to create an Old Testament society which made ambition difficult, so the Son did the same.

Jesus had very little time for volunteers. He never appealed for them. He never asked whether there was anyone in the crowd who was interested in following him. Just as God had chosen the judges, so Jesus chose his followers. He simply went up to selected individuals and said, 'Follow me.' Those who did volunteer, like the men in Luke 9:57–62, were not commended; I think Jesus found their presumption distasteful. And, as in John 15:16, he crushed any developing ambition in his disciples by frequently reminding them, 'You did not choose me, no, I chose you.'

He abolished offices, so that ambition for prestige, position, prominence and advancement should not exist among his followers. Passages like Matthew 18:4; 20:20–28; 23:8–12; Mark 9:33–37; 10:41–45; Luke 9:46–48; 14:7–11; 17:7–10; 22:24–27; and John 13:1–16 make this quite plain. Yet who takes these verses seriously today? We must. I think that every minister should have them emblazoned across his desk.

Jesus made self-denial an absolute condition of following him. In Luke 9:23 he said to the twelve disciples, people who had already been called to follow him and who were experienced miracle workers, 'If anyone wants to be a follower of mine, let him renounce himself and take up his cross every day and follow me.' Similar sentiments are recorded in Matthew 16:24; Mark 8:34; and Luke 14:33. Surely this must be the reverse of presumption and ambition: to renounce oneself regularly, consciously, carefully, and deliberately?

Jesus' command to those who already are his followers—and this means you and me—is that every day, in every situation, we must, as an act of our will, choose to deny ourselves, to renounce our intentions and ambitions, and pick up our cross—the symbol of our imminent death. This means that we must live every day as if we really are a part of Christ's body on earth; it means that in everything we must restrict our thinking, our speaking and our actions to those few things which Christ has expressly instructed; and we must live every day with the same clear understanding, attitude and concerns as the condemned man who knows he will hang before breakfast the next day. In this lies the freedom from fear and worry which is abundant life.

Christ demanded that his followers depend on the Father's provision in the same way he did. Matthew 6:19, 24–34; Luke 9:3; 10:3–8; and 12:13–34 apply this to material needs, and Luke 24:49 shows it spiritually. The Old Testament judges and prophets were first chosen by God, and then were given the gift of God's Spirit as the convincing evidence of their calling and the necessary equipment for it. God followed the same pattern with Jesus himself; and it was to be repeated in the experience of Christ's followers. Jesus had chosen them, and after his ascension they were to wait until Jesus gave them the equipment that the Father had promised. They were not to presume that their three years of experience with him had been adequate training. They must attempt nothing without the gift, and they could do nothing to earn it. They simply had to ensure that they were in God's right place at God's right time.

There are few things as incongruous as an ambitious

man or woman who professes to have received the gift of God's Holy Spirit. The Holy Spirit exists to give glory to another. He delights in anonymity. He is so self-effacing that he has recorded few incidents or details about himself. He is such a mystery that we have to use metaphors to describe him. And Jesus, who was filled with Holy Spirit, exhibited all these characteristics of the Spirit. Jesus ordered demons and disciples alike not to tell people that he was the Christ. He told those who had been healed to remain silent about the source of their cure. He sought neither crowds nor popularity. He shows—as Gideon had been shown hundreds of years earlier—that quality is more important than quantity. He valued silence, secrecy, brevity, patience and quiet persistence. Oh, what does he make of his followers today?

After thirty long years of quiet, unassuming preparation, and three years of the most authoritative evangelistic campaign, the wisest teaching ministry, and one of the most prolific demonstrations of 'signs and wonders' that the world will ever see, Jesus died. He had been rejected, ridiculed, despised, misrepresented and physically abused. Fewer than five hundred people believed in him. His treasurer had betrayed him. His lieutenant had deserted him. If only he had been a little bit ambitious he might have achieved more. If only he had organised himself better, used proper publicity, asked for volunteers, and seized the opportunities which the cheering crowds so often presented, if only he had not wasted so many years working as a carpenter, why, many more people might have believed in him.

But that was not, and is not, God's way. All our thoughts about ambition, all our so-called 'good' intentions for our lives, our families, our businesses, even—God forgive us—our congregations, all of these have to be measured against the life and death of Jesus Christ. Are we presumptuous volunteers who, like our enemy, are soon dissatisfied with our circumstances, regularly seek self-fulfilment, and superficially prosper because of our ambition? Or are we chosen people who, like our leader, will depend on God's provision, deny ourselves daily, and devote our lives to inconspicuous service?

We will now examine the path taken by the church in New Testament times, and attempt to apply these scriptural principles to our current situation.

Ambition Opposed

You cannot belong to Christ Jesus unless you crucify all self-indulgent passions and desires.

St Paul

None of Jesus' four younger brothers appears to have followed him before the Resurrection. However, one of them became the leader of the Jerusalem Christians for nearly thirty years and had unparalleled authority in the early church. Towards the end of his life James wrote a pastoral letter to scattered Jewish Christians which contains one of the clearest scriptural denunciations of ambition.

James 3:13–17 is remarkably similar to 1 Samuel 15:23 when it says of selfish ambition, 'Principles of this kind are not the wisdom that comes down from above: they are only earthly, animal and devilish. Wherever you find jealousy and ambition, you find disharmony, and wicked things of every kind being done.'

Some people suggest that the adjective 'self-seeking' in verse 14 is a qualification of ambition and that, therefore, a commendable form of unselfish ambition must exist. But they are grasping at a straw to justify their own ambition, for to be consistent they must also advocate a type of jealousy which is not bitter, and they must somehow explain away the simplicity of verse 17. James' word 'self-seeking' (NIV, 'selfish'), does not qualify ambition, but graphically underlines its essential nature. It's the same as calling grass green and water wet.

In the early days of the church God condemned ambition in a startling and awesome manner. Acts 5:1–11 tells the story of how one couple's ambition for a good reputation and public acclamation ended in their death. Verse 11 states, 'This made a profound impression on the whole Church.' Nothing could have more clearly underlined God's opposition to ambition.

The apostle Paul had to learn the lesson that his Lord was fundamentally opposed to presumption. In Acts 16:6–10 he was given clear instructions by the Holy Spirit not to preach in Asia. But when he reached the Mysian frontier 'he thought' to cross into Bithynia, probably intending to head for Byzantium. Paul's presumption in going where he thought rather than waiting for God's instructions met with divine opposition; in some way God intervened, and Paul headed west for Troas.

Paul appears to have learnt from this incident, as no presumption can be detected after the Mysian frontier episode. In Acts 18:20–21 we read that when he left the Ephesians he said, 'I will come back another time, God willing.' Paul was planning a return but did not presume that it would inevitably occur. He used similar language in Romans 15:32, and again in 1 Corinthians 16:5–9, where his phrase 'the Lord permitting' indicates his lack of presumption.

The relationship between planning and presumption is the same as that between desire and ambition. Planning and desire are only sinful if their objects are sinful, but if they develop into presumption or ambition they automatically become evil—even if the object of ambition or presumption is good.

James makes this plain in two passages. In James

1:13–15 he shows that desire is not necessarily sinful in itself, but that it may lead on to sin. And in 4:13–15 James does not criticise planning, but lashes out at presumption, 'The most you should ever say is: "If it is the Lord's will, we shall be alive to do this or that."'

James illustrates this principle by highlighting and condemning one particular act of presumption. In James 3:14 he writes, 'never make any claims for yourself'. Although James could have described himself as the brother of Jesus and leader of the church for over a quarter of a century, he chose to introduce himself in James 1:1 simply as 'servant of God and of the Lord Jesus Christ'. Those Christian leaders who issue curricula vitae which stress all that *they* have done, *their* outstanding healing ministry, *their* international teaching ministry, or the rapid growth in *their* church due to *their* inspired leadership presume too much. They need reminding that James considers such claims to be 'earthly, animal and devilish'.

Paul makes a similar point. In Colossians 2:18 he warns against those 'who inflate themselves to a false importance' and are 'always going on about some vision they have had'. And in Romans 12:3 he pleads, 'I want to urge each one among you not to exaggerate his real importance.' This sentence is set in a passage which stresses the body and the inter-dependence of Christians. When Paul's 'body' analogy is considered it can be seen at once that spiritual ambition is nonsense. Can one leg become more prominent than the other? Can the left hand pretend to be more vital than the right eye? Can the stomach intend to become a lung when it grows older? It is patently absurd. Although such notions are impossible within a human body, the freedom God gives believers makes such ambitions attainable within the body of Christ. I find it strange that the recent emphasis on the 'body' has not led to the obvious conclusion that congregational and personal ambition are both as dangerous and destructive as cancer.

In Romans 2:1–4 Paul mentions another unpalatable piece of presumption which still prevails today. 'So no matter who you are, if you pass judgement you have no excuse. In judging others you condemn yourself, since you behave no differently from those you judge... do you think you will escape God's judgement?' To presume to judge is to usurp God's exclusive function. Jesus taught that only those who are without sin may judge. Yet our religious press is full of presumptuous judgements; our Christian conversations are riddled with malicious gossip; and our ministers' retreats are soured by ignorant criticism. We are ambitious to impress, to put down, to be listened to, and so we are without excuse. We will not escape God's judgement. Our reward will not be great in the kingdom of heaven.

Paul's example is as clear as his teaching. Acts 13:2–3 describes how he and Barnabas believed that they had been called by God to preach in Barnabas' native country. In spite of this, at first they did not budge one inch from Antioch. They made their plans, but did not presume. They were waiting for a much clearer and more general indication as to whether and when they should leave. Yet many today justify their activity by insisting, 'God has told *me*': they presume God has spoken; they presume he has given a command rather than a promise; and they presume he means at once. But Paul was more patient than we are. He knew that David had had to wait fifteen years after his anointing by Samuel before he became king of Israel. And Paul understood the significance of Jesus' long wait before beginning to preach.

Acts 8:18–23 is a relevant story. Simon had been astonished by the signs and wonders that he had seen. He had received Holy Spirit, had noted the association between this and involvement in the miraculous, and was ambitious to be able to lay his hands on people indiscriminately so that they would also receive Holy Spirit. Because Simon naively thought money could purchase the power he was first rebuked by Peter, and then was reminded that this ability was given by God for nothing. Few today think they can buy a ministry from God; but many forget the gift principle and, being ambitious for power, try to earn this ministry: they read a book, attend a conference, visit a particular church, fast, pray, and so on. We are encouraged earnestly to desire the spiritual gifts, but that is a very different matter from presuming that there is something we can do to ensure that we receive them.

Romans 12:6–8; 1 Corinthians 4:7; and 1 Corinthians 12–14 unite in demanding that the early church understand the significance of the word 'gift'. A giver has the right to give his gifts both when he pleases and to whom he pleases. Sensible beggars may position themselves near someone they know to be generous; they may stretch out their hands; they may smile and say please; they may express their needs and earnest desires; they may even be optimistic about the outcome of their request. But they dare not presume.

To talk of being ambitious for a gift is a contradiction in terms, yet many today believe that they are 'spiritual' if they are ambitious for a gift of God. Even worse, some presume that those who have not been given a gift must be 'unspiritual'. A gift is a gift; it is not a reward. There is not necessarily anything virtuous about those who do receive, and nothing necessarily iniquitous about those who do not.

The leaders of the early church exhorted the believers to remember some vital principles which, if applied, would help them crucify all ambition.

Firstly, Romans 1:1; 8:28–30; 1 Corinthians 1:26–29; Galatians 1:15; Ephesians 1:4 and 2 Peter 1:10 emphasise the truth that all Christians are called and chosen by God alone. When we remember that almighty God himself has selected us for a particular form of service how can we ever have the audacity even to want to do something else, let alone attempt to do something different? If Jesus, with all his potential, was happy with the calling of a carpenter, then surely his followers can be content in their chosen calling.

Secondly, in Acts 20:17–36; 1 Corinthians 1:27–29; 4:10–13; and 2 Corinthians 12:10 Paul stresses that he is 'the offal of the world... the scum of the earth' and that all those who follow Jesus are nothing. 'Those whom the world thinks common and contemptible are the ones that God has chosen—those who are nothing at all...' Nothing cannot be ambitious to be anything; only God can transform nothing into something. If Jesus was not ambitious for anything other than his lot of rejection, contempt, poverty and suffering, then neither should those who profess to worship and follow him. True disciples will rejoice with those who are rejected, not offer them inner healing; they will be content with their personal poverty, not construe it as a mark of sin; and they will embrace suffering, not pray that it goes away.

Furthermore, in Philippians 3:8 Paul writes, 'I have accepted the loss of everything, and I look on everything as so much rubbish if only I can have Christ.' He was ambitious for nothing, and rejoiced in losing everything, because he knew that Christ was better than anything. If he had nothing he therefore had more room, more time and more energy for Christ. Two verses later he writes, 'All I want is to know Christ and the power of his resurrection and to share his sufferings...' Many today covet the power. Few desire the sufferings.

Thirdly, both Paul and Peter urge their readers to be self-effacing. Ephesians 5:21–6:9; Philippians 2:2–4; and 1 Peter 3:8 urge mutual submission as the truly Christian lifestyle: 'Give way to one another in obedience to Christ.' 'Everybody is to be self-effacing. Always consider the other person to be better than yourself, so that nobody thinks of his own interests first.' 'Agree among yourselves and be sympathetic; love the brothers, have compassion and be self-effacing.' If this apostolic command were obeyed, ambition would be eliminated from the church.

Fourthly, 1 Timothy 6:17; 2 Timothy 4:3; Hebrews 13:5; and 2 Peter 1:3 ask that believers 'be content': content with God's financial provision for us as he, 'out of his riches, gives us all that we need for our happiness'; and content with the spiritual teaching he has provided for us at a time when 'people will be avid for the latest novelty, and collect themselves a whole series of teachers according to their own tastes'. If discontentment is the root of all ambition it is only to be expected that followers of Jesus will be ordered to be content; for the man or woman who is truly content will never commit the original sin. Why, then, do we encourage discontentment?

Finally, as Christ had instructed the twelve, the early church were urged to renounce themselves and take up their cross daily. The apostles set the example by renouncing their reputation. Acts 5:40–41 tells how, after having been flogged, they were 'glad to have had the honour of suffering humiliation for the sake of the name'. Stephen, in his turn, renounced his life. Acts 6:8–8:2 reports how this financial administrator who had worked miracles whilst distributing food to the poor, was arrested, tried and executed. Philip renounced his public success. Acts 8:4–26 shows how, in the midst of an amazingly successful signs, wonders and evangelistic campaign in Samaria, he set off for an apparently pointless visit to the desert.

And Barnabas renounced his position as leader. Acts 13 traces how the relationship changed from 'Barnabas and Saul' at the start of their journey to 'Paul and Barnabas' by the time they left Paphos. Barnabas had graciously stepped down from being the missionary leader and Saul's tutor, and had willingly become Paul's subordinate and deputy.

To me Barnabas is the archetype of the unambitious leader: he never presumed, never made claims about himself, only looked for ways of encouraging others. When Saul, the once fanatical Pharisee, returned to Jerusalem from Damascus, and started preaching about Jesus, Barnabas did not prejudge Saul, but risked his life to discover whether Saul had actually been converted. Barnabas remembered that he had been called and chosen, he knew he was nothing and did not mind when he lost his prominent position. He was as content to be last as he had been happy to be first. He had no need to read Paul's words in Philippians 2:5: 'In your minds you must be the same as Christ Jesus.'

Jesus was the model for the early church, and he must be our example today. Many people long to be like the powerful preaching, healing, exorcising, miracle-working King of kings. Some groups now even name their congregations 'The King's church'. But that was not what Paul had in mind. 'He emptied himself to assume the condition of a slave... and was humbler yet, even to accepting death, death on a cross.' When congregations call themselves 'the Servant's church' or 'the Slave's church' they will have begun to be like those first believers who emulated the Poor Man of Galilee, the Suffering Servant, the Sacrificial Lamb. That unassuming, self-effacing, unambitious slave is the God we need to learn from, imitate and follow.

Ambition Crucified

The world is saying to the Church: Unless I see in your hands the print of the nails, I will not believe.

G Campbell Morgan

Ambition has come a long way since its malevolent premiere in heaven. It has grown tentacles, which have spread throughout all mankind. And the evil being who committed that opening sin continues to use ambition as his basic weapon in his fight against the world and the church. Only one man has ever succeeded in completely resisting its suffocating stranglehold, but all his followers can experience something of his freedom from ambition's deadly grip.

Today, Christians use words like racialism, sexual deviancy, violence and materialism to describe the tentacles which grip the world, without realising that these words are only fancy pseudonyms for ambition. We are always good at denouncing sins which we think we are unlikely to commit. But surely the ambition for self-gratification we condemn as homosexuality is no different from the ambition for self-gratification encouraged at the Christian meetings which people attend to get a kick out of spiritual activity. Surely the ambition for superiority which we reject as racialism is no worse than the ambition for congregational or denominational superiority which is passed off as Christian doctrine from so many platforms and pulpits. And surely what we acclaim as vision in our leaders is often the same as the devilish appetite for personal achievement we so loathe in our politicians.

This is nothing new. As far back as the sixteenth century St John of the Cross was inspired to write extensively, in *Dark Night of the Soul*, about the spiritual versions of the seven deadly sins. And since then the Catholic branch of the church has admonished every hint of ambition. But part of our evangelical heritage from the Puritans is the assumption that ambition, especially a supposedly spiritual form of ambition, is an acceptable state of mind. Charles Finney's mid-nineteenth century *Lectures on Systematic Theology* powerfully repudiated that line of thought, but few people read Finney today.

Sadly, the spirit of the Thatcher era has greatly influenced the English church. Many ministers have unwittingly been affected by the extraordinary social, political, educational and media emphases on independence, advancement, attainment, success, prosperity and so on. We live in an age when Satan has hoodwinked most believers into thinking that the very first sin has turned into a virtue. We exist at a time when contented believers are frequently made to feel uncomfortable, unspiritual and second-rate. And we are now part of a church which sacks and ostracises those ministers who confess to an occasional sexual sin, but which applauds and rewards those who proudly flaunt their many ambitions. How Satan must laugh!

Paul teaches in Galatians 5:24 that we cannot belong to Christ unless we crucify all self-indulgent passions and desires. He does not say that we should stop being self-indulgent. He does not say that we should ask God to take our self-indulgence away. He does not say we should thank God that Christ's work on the cross has set us free from self-indulgence. No, Paul uses the hideous metaphor of crucifixion, and he puts all responsibility for carrying out the self-crucifixion on our shoulders.

We have to pick up the cross. We have to stumble under its weight to the place of execution. We have to dig the hole and drop the gibbet in. We have to climb on to the scaffold. And, somehow, we have to hammer the nails into our own wrists. Then we must go on hanging there until our self-indulgent ambition shrivels and falls away.

Some folk point to Galatians 2:20 and say that all this talk about self-crucifixion is quite unnecessary. They maintain that we have already been crucified with Christ as a direct consequence of our spiritual union with him by faith. They prefer crucifixion by faith to crucifixion by nails: so do I; but, sadly, it is not what Paul is referring to.

Galatians 5:24 and 2:20 teach complementary truths. By faith we have shared in Christ's crucifixion, and the benefit to us from that death is a freedom from the law's condemnation which enables us to live by faith in God's Son. But we also have actively to crucify our self, and the benefit from this death is a freedom from our sinful selfish nature which liberates us to be led by God's Spirit.

So those of us who think we belong to him, especially those of us who stress being led by the Spirit, had better start crucifying all ambition. I believe it is critical for the church to recognise ambition for the selfish sin that it is; and to name it, and to go on naming it, as undiluted sin. Those who are called to preach need consistently to proclaim the absolute incompatibility of ambition and

Christian discipleship. Sermon after sermon is wasted in a torrent of words which lambast sins irrelevant to those seated on the pews and plastic chairs, while ambition continues unchecked.

We should feel acute shame when we detect ambition —whatever its form or object—in our lives and in our congregations. We should be far more offended and embarrassed by a Christian who presumes to say 'I will' or 'we will' than we are by an unbeliever who blasphemes in our presence. We should pray that those Christian leaders who reek of unbridled ambition, for themselves and for their congregations, may be convicted of their sin and summon up the courage to crucify all their ambition and tread the path of self-denial. Those with responsibility for recognising and appointing the people whom God has chosen to be ministers, elders, deacons, house-group leaders, and so on, should resist the temptation to prefer the ambitious, and remember that God favours the meek. And together we must become a community of called and chosen people who not only recognise ambition as intrinsically evil, but are also intransigently opposed to its insidious presence in our midst.

I make the following practical suggestions for our self-crucifixion, praying that they will be both helpful and relevant as daily we renounce ourselves, take up our cross, and follow Christ.

We must reject competition. In Philippians 2:3 Paul commands that, 'There must be no competition between you.' So why does blatant competition exist between ministers, evangelists, congregations, Bible weeks, denominations and societies? In the same verse Paul states, 'Always consider the other person to be better than yourself.' Yet advertisements, brochures, leaflets, public statements and private conversations usually imply, and occasionally scream, 'Come to us, we're the best'; 'Listen to me, I'm God's man of the moment'; 'Don't go elsewhere, it can't be as good as here'. Competition is ambition in disguise; no matter how subtle, it always denies the doctrine of Christ's single body. It must be eliminated from our churches and our personal lives.

We must reject presumption. We presume that a large congregation is a sign of blessing. We presume that we are right. We presume that our form of worship is God's favourite. We presume that leaders and members of other denominations would benefit greatly from listening to us and attending our meetings. We presume that bigger is better. We presume that God wants us to be successful. We presume that whatever we are involved with is very significant. We presume that our ideas are God's direction. We presume that God wants everything to happen instantly. And, worst of all, we presume that our presumption is faith.

It is a dangerous teaching which suggests that to ask in faith means to pray only once, and then shut up and pretend that God has supplied what was asked for. That is presumption, not faith. Such teaching relegates God from a giver to a vendor, and ignores the biblical links between faith and patience, and prayer and perseverance. Faith means going on asking, going on believing, going on struggling, even when circumstances suggest that God is absent or impotent. Presumption asks no questions, heeds no delays, and denies God's sovereignty.

Both personally and corporately, we must stop making

claims about ourselves, and ask others not to make claims on our behalf. Jesus did not brag about the people he had healed, resuscitated, exorcised and saved. So why do we? Paul does not list his miracles in 2 Corinthians 6. So why do we? In his passage on boasting, in 2 Corinthians 11 and 12, Paul writes, 'If I am to boast, then let me boast of my own feebleness' (11:30). When will we do the same?

We spend millions of pounds on advertising and self-publicity, whilst our third world brothers and sisters starve to death: it is obscene. We believe in slick publicity, regular press releases, expensive advertising campaigns, and blowing our own trumpets. Yet as we have seen, Jesus came in anonymity, to live in obscurity, to die in agony, alone. He commanded silence, sought solitude, embraced suffering, and delighted in secrecy. We delight in attention, ache for ever-increasing crowds, fast for success, and pray for the day when the media gives us prime time coverage—on our terms. How Jesus weeps! Surely it is time we shredded the brochures and videos which publicise our successes and ignore our failures in an attempt to attract attention and money. Surely it is time we silenced the devilish claims about *our*selves, *our* congregations, and *our* ministries. Surely it is time we started talking about our *feebleness*, our *weakness*, and our *ignorance*. Only then will we be people who have begun to crucify all ambition.

We must reject worldly thinking and learn from the Old Testament battles that victory does not depend on larger numbers, superior weapons, or more astute tactics. Yet in recent years there has been a great emphasis on the importance of ecclesiastical aims, goals, strategy, methodology and equipment. Scholars have studied growing congregations and isolated what they deem to be common causal factors. So ministers now attend courses to learn how to make their congregations grow. Blinded by their ambition, they foolishly believe that there must be a formula for success, and are ensnared into thinking that growth is a right rather than a gift.

And, lastly, I think that we must stop being preoccupied with the future, and start living in the present. Ambition presupposes that tomorrow is more important than today. A competitive attitude, a presumptive frame of mind, an over-emphasis on planning, a stress on good publicity, endless talking about visions of the future, all of these betray that we are besotted with tomorrow; but Jesus taught that we should take up our cross daily. If we really believed this we, like all condemned men, would not be over-concerned with the future.

This is not to suggest that planning is necessarily wrong: as with desire, it is only evil when the object is sinful. James 4:15 strikes the balance. The old-fashioned use of DV (the popular abbreviation of the latin phrase *deo volente*, 'God being willing') was rather twee, but when sincerely meant it was exactly right. I believe that we need to discover a modern counterpart to DV which is easily understood by contemporary people, and which communicates a sincere and holy hesitation.

All of these suggestions have been made to help us hammer the nails into our personal and congregational ambition. And, in one sense, Part One of this trilogy should end here, at the Good Friday of our ambition. But we know that death is not the end. The message, if not the reality, of Easter Sunday is well known. The next and final chapter really belongs to Part Three of this trilogy, but the news is so good, and what has come before has been so depressing, that I am unable to resist including a brief glimpse of the glory awaiting those resurrected, ambition-free corpses which stumble along in step with the Spirit.

Free From Ambition

Almighty God,
whose most dear Son went not up to joy
but first suffered pain,
and entered not into glory before he was crucified;
mercifully grant that we,
walking in the way of the cross,
may find it none other than the way of life
and peace;
through Jesus Christ our Lord.

Collect for the third Sunday in Lent in the
Church of England's Alternative Service Book.

All the suggestions made in the last chapter were different ways of ensuring that ambition is crucified and removed from the life of the church. But the God of the resurrection calls us out of our graves and commissions us, as liberated corpses, to live by faith in his Son, and to be led at all times by his Spirit. That has to be glorious.

If our only existence is in Christ it must mean we go where he goes, think what he thinks, love whom he loves, act as he acts, value what he values, befriend the unlikely, say the surprising, do the improbable, become unpredictable, and share in his rejection, suffering and eventual glory.

And if our desire is to keep in step with the Spirit it must mean that we wander with him down his pathway of quiet persistence, gentle encouragement, unpretentious modesty and holy anonymity; that we emulate him by ensuring we fend off every attempt to focus any attention on ourselves; that, like him, we neither seek nor make any record of our own activities; and that filled with him, empowered by him, and becoming ever more like him, we choose to live not to gain glory for ourselves, but to give glory to others.

I am sure this means that self-denial must become the dominant characteristic in our lives. Self-denial is the glorious virtue that ambition has usurped; it is the glory we need to recognise and embrace; it is the definitive Christian way of life. (Part Three of this trilogy examines the relationship between glory and sacrifice in some detail, and offers a fuller description of a positive way forward.) The expression 'self-denial' is shorthand for the much longer phrase 'the crucified lifestyle of the person who both lives in Christ and is led by the Spirit'. It is the application of the spiritual principle that the follower of Jesus has no rights because he has relinquished all rights. It is elementary spiritual logic:

1. God became a human slave.
2. In our thinking we are to be like him.
3. A slave has no rights.
4. So neither have we.

However, a slave may receive gifts; and he does have certain duties which must be performed. Some people suggest that the only alternative to ambition is apathy, but inactivity is itself a form of ambition for self-indulgence. Surely apathetic inactivity is a modern name for sloth, one of the 'seven deadly sins'. We may be called to be nothing, but we are not called to do nothing; for we are slaves, servants, and stewards. We may be overlooked, underpaid and apparently worthless, but we are called to be content with our nothingness and to get on with whatever work God has given us to do, making the best use we can of our God-given talents.

The central vow of the annual Methodist Covenant service expresses this particularly well. Each person present says,

> I am no longer my own, but yours. Put me to what you will, rank me with whom you will; put me to doing, put me to

> suffering; let me be employed for you or laid aside for you, exalted for you or brought low for you; let me be full, let me be empty; let me have all things, let me have nothing; I freely and wholeheartedly yield all things to your pleasure and disposal. And now, glorious and blessed God, Father, Son, and Holy Spirit, you are mine and I am yours. So be it. And the covenant now made on earth, let it be ratified in heaven. Amen.

Self-denial is positive, God-initiated, action which begins in personal contentment. Once again the Methodist Covenant service illustrates this: just before the people make their annual vow the minister says to them, 'To take his yoke upon us means that we are content that he appoint us our place and work, and that he himself be our reward.' Christ's clear but uncomfortable commands of Matthew 5:13—7:29 begin in personal happiness. If self-denial is not rooted in a state of contented happiness it inevitably becomes the loveless legalism rejected by Paul as worthless in 1 Corinthians 13:3.

We are called to be content with God's provision in every area of our lives: our ability and talents, our location and work, our finance, our family, our friends, our congregation, and so on. Of course, this does not mean that we are to be content with sin in our lives, as this is not something which God has provided. Nor should we be apathetic towards rampant evil in society, as God might call us to speak or act about it. But we should be content with God's provision of forgiveness to deal with our sin, and not try to do things—or go without things—to earn his forgiveness. And we should be content with God's direction that we live, work and witness in society surrounded by its rampant evil, and not try to do things to escape, or help our children escape, from the proximity of evil.

Scripture is packed with God's promises—some conditional and many unconditional—and we have the glorious privilege of reading them, receiving them, being content with them, and being made content by them. Some people construe a promise as a command; others boast about a promise as though it were a reward for their good behaviour; and many more are unsettled by a promise, forgetting that with God a day is as a thousand years: his understanding of 'soon' appears to be very different from our own! If God has clearly made a promise it needs to be silently filed away, not widely broadcast; it needs to be constantly remembered, not presumptuously self-fulfilled; and normal life must continue, tinged now with the certain light of hope. When God has said 'let there be' we know that it will be, but we don't know when it will be. Much of our lives is spent in the faith-stretching tension between the divine 'let there be' and the human 'it was so'.

We must learn to value stillness, silence and serving God secretly. But above all we must begin to see the importance of making loving sacrifices. Sacrifices always appear to be irresponsible, unnecessary, foolish, meaningless, wasteful, and out of step with the spirit of this age. Today we would lock up anybody who tried to do what Abraham started to do to Isaac. We would attempt to dissuade anyone who proposed to marry the same sort of person as Hosea. And if a new convert asked whether he should copy Zacchaeus we'd tell him that it was quite unnecessary. But the cross is central to our faith. Loving, God-initiated sacrifices are what please our Father most. They are of incalculable worth to him; they are what he esteems most highly.

I think of the experienced minister who resigned from his flourishing five hundred-strong church to care for a congregation of twelve; the retired couple who have allocated two rooms and much time to receive and love a stream of unconverted pregnant teenagers; and the mum who, without complaining or receiving any thanks, runs the creche and misses the services week after week after week. These are the real heroes of the modern-day church, not those whose glossy photos and ghost-written books adorn the pages of the religious press.

I remember the friend who refused promotion because it meant moving, and he would not abandon his small Sunday school class; the rapidly growing congregation which, instead of building bigger barns or creating an empire, asked half its members to join existing, struggling, local congregations of other denominations; and the over-looked old couple who dust the pews and mow the grass without minding that nobody notices their loyalty. These are those who have sacrificed their ambitions and embraced obscurity to follow the sacrificial Lamb.

I echo God's applause for the talented missionary who left a thriving work to return home and care for her aged parents; for the middle class family who strengthened a weak congregation by moving from suburbia to the inner city; and for the frustrated family who resisted the temptation to follow the exodus of friends from apparently dismal denominational churches into the superficially super new fellowship round the corner.

These are the people we should learn from, imitate, and invite to speak at our meetings. These are those who have shared in Christ's defeat of ambition, who in their thinking are truly like Christ the slave, who obey their Lord and take up their cross, daily. These are the members of that holy company whose slender ranks we must join, so that the opening sin can be crucified and permanently erased from the lives of those who profess to follow Christ.